If you were me and lived in...

POLAND

A Child's Introduction to Culture Around the World

Carole P. Roman

Illustrated by Kelsea Wierenga

For Feiga, Kalman, Bianca, and Minca

Special thanks to Ewa R. for all her help.

Copyright © 2013 Carole P. Roman

All rights reserved.

ISBN-10: 1-947118-80-3

ISBN-13: 978-1-947118-80-5

Disclaimer:
Please note that there may be differences in dialect that will vary according to region. Multiple individuals (from each country) were used as sources for the pronunciation key but you should be aware of the possibility of alternative pronunciations.

POLAND

If you were me and lived in Poland, you would find yourself in Central Europe (Ur-rup) in a country you called Pokska (Pol-ska), but the rest of the world called it the Republic of Poland (Pol-land). People from Poland are called Polanie (Po-la-kee). The name Polanie means people living in open field.

The Kingdom of Poland was founded in the year 1025.

The Polish constitution (con-ste-to-tion) was written on May 3, 1791, making it the first in Europe and second in the world.

You might live in the capital of Warsaw (Var-shav-a). Warsaw was built on the banks of the Wisla (Vee-swa) River. Outside of Poland, people call it the Vistula (Vis-jula) River, and it is located in the central eastern part of Poland.

There is a legend that Warsaw got its name from a fisherman named Wars (Wars), who fell in love with a mermaid who lived in the river. Her name was Sawa (Sa-va). Because of this legend, there are many statues of mermaids in the city. There is a mermaid on the official city seal.

You would love to explore the beautiful city and sometimes get tired from all that walking. When you sit down on one of the black stone benches, make sure you press the button on it. You will get a sample of Fryderyk Chopin's (Fred-drik Jou-paen) music. He was Poland's most important and famous composer in the 1800s.

If you are a boy, your parents might have chosen the name Marek (Mar-ek), Filip (Feel-ip), or Jakub (Ya-coob). They could have picked the name Weronika (Ver-on-nee-ka), Ewa (Av-a), or Karolina (Kar-o-leen-a) for your sister.

Mama (Ma-ma) has a special nickname for your sister. She calls her kotkczo (kot-tek) or kittycat. Your father, Tata (Tata), says you are his little misiek (meesh-ek) because you enjoy rolling around like a bear cub.

When you go to the sklep (skl-ep) with Mama, she would use zloty (zwa-te) when she buys mleko (mle-ko) and chleb (hleb) for your lunch. You would remind her not to forget the szynca (shin-ka) and ser (ser) for your sandwich. Where do you think you are? Can you guess what are the names for milk, bread, ham and cheese?

Your favorite vacation would always be to visit the Wielicza (Via-lech-ka) Salt Mine located on the outskirts of Krakow (Krac-kof). Salt was mined there continuously since the thirteenth century up until 2007. It was one of the oldest companies in the world. Now it is a great tourist attraction. In the olden days, salt was essential for curing meat and valuable for trading. What makes this place special is the unique underground city completely carved from rock salt by the miners who worked there over hundreds of years. There is a chapel (cha-pel) that is said to have the best acoustics (a-cous-tics) of any other structure in Europe. That means when music is played there, it bounces off the walls to surround you in sound. Ancient sculptures stand side by side with new and modern carvings that have been added.

Sunday you always visit Babcia (Bob-cha) and Dziadek (Jah-dik) on their farm.

Babcia gets up early to prepare all of your favorite foods. She starts dinner with rosol (ro-sool) broth. This is a chicken soup with loads of carrots, celery, onions, leek, dill, and homemade noodles called makaron (mac-kar-on). She would serve platters of golabki (go-um-kee), which are tasty cabbage leaves stuffed with ground pork and rice. Tata loves sledz (sle-je) marinated with cebula (ceb-u-la), which is a pickled herring and sliced onion in a cream sauce. You prefer the hearty meat stew called bigos (bee-gos), packed with sausages, prunes, onions, and tasty mushrooms called grzybki (gribp-kee). Everybody fights over the last pierogi (peer-rog-gee) because the potato filled pockets of dough are the best in the world.

You finish the meal with chrusciki (chus-chee-kee), the delicate bows of light pastry dusted with white sugar.

Most kids don't play with traditional toys, preferring to spend their free time outdoors bird-watching, sledding, or playing sports. Your sister would still bring along her lalka (lal-ka). Can you guess what that is?

Everybody knows that the most popular sport in Poland is football, which is called pilka nozna (peu-ka noz-nah).

You never miss a game of ice hockey.

Last year, Mama and Tata took you skiing, and you had so much fun going down the learner's hill.

You do love bird-watching with your grandfather. Poland is famous in that of all the migratory (my-gra-tor-ee) birds that travel to Europe for the summer, one quarter of them breed in Poland, making it the most important bird breeding ground in Europe.

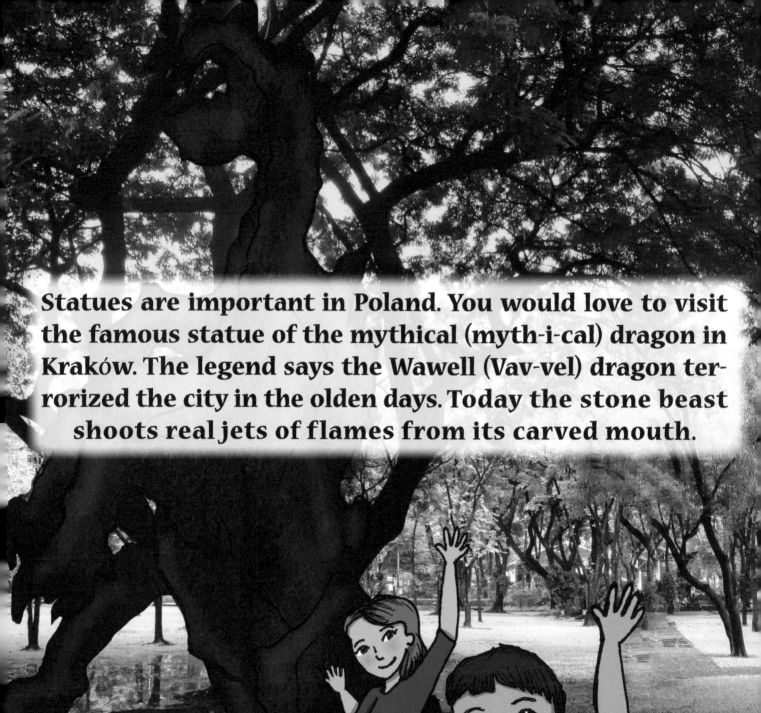

Statues are important in Poland. You would love to visit the famous statue of the mythical (myth-i-cal) dragon in Kraków. The legend says the Wawell (Vav-vel) dragon terrorized the city in the olden days. Today the stone beast shoots real jets of flames from its carved mouth.

There is a nice game to play in Wroclaw (Vroz-swaf). It is a pastime called "spot the gnome (nom)." While you are seeing all the cathedrals, market squares, and the picturesque waterways, you will also look for those little pesky creatures that do annoying tricks. When someone spots one, you make sure to take a photo of these little hard-working guys. You search for them on almost all objects of the city such as sitting on lampposts, hanging from doorways, and perched on benches.

Children's Day or Dzien Dziecka (Jen Jet-ska) is a special day in Poland. It is celebrated on June 1st. Parents buy chocolates and gifts to honor this joyous day of recognition of children. Schools organize fun outdoor activities, and it is a day of exciting things to do. It is the best day in the world for children!

Some children will be lucky enough to be included in a special session of the government's parliament (par-lee-ment) or sejm (same). They are given the opportunity to learn about and discuss world issues.

You love to learn about Nicolaus Copernicus (Nik-co-lai Cop-per-nik), the famous 16th century astronomer (as-tron-o-mer). He was born in Poland and revolutionized the way the world looked at the solar system. He said the earth actually circled the sun, rather than the other way around. This was a completely new idea and was a impor-tant contribution to science.

Upon his father's ... under his wing and saw ... ures in Poland and was a f... si.[45] There are no surviving p... pernicus biographers assume that Wa... himself had been a master.[9] Later, accor... up the Vistula River from Toruń, which prepar... alma mater in Poland's capital.[46]

In the winter semester of 1491–92 Copernicus, as "Nicolaus ... brother Andrew at the University of Kraków (now Jagiel... Department of Arts (from the fall of 1491, presumably ... astronomical-mathematical school, acquiring the fo... cording to a later but credible tradition (Jan Broż... (from 1491) was a professor of Aristotelian phil... eus became familiar with Brudzewski's widel... and almost certainly attended the lectures of... other astronomical lectures by Jan of Gło... of Olkusz.[47]

Copernicus' ... studies gave hi... th... geomet... pl...

Nicolaus Copernicus

You would learn all about Copernicus in szkola (scko-wa).
Can you guess where that is?

So you see, if you were me, how life in Poland could really be.

Pronunciation Guide

acoustics (a-cous-tics)- sound quality often made better by the way the noise bounces off its surroundings.

astronomer (as-tron-o-mer)- someone who studies the night sky.

Babcia (Bob-cha)- Grandmother.

bigos (bee-gos)- hearty stew filled with sausages, meats, prunes, onions, and mushrooms.

cebula (ceb-u-la)- onions.

chapel (chap-el)- a part of a house or building dedicated to religion and prayer.

chleb (hleb)- bread.

chrusciki (chus-chee-kee)- fried bows of crispy dough that are dusted with sugar.

constitution (con-ste-to-tion)- a set of laws that govern a land.

Dzien Dziecka (Jen-jet-ska)- Children's Day- a national holiday celebrated June 1st.

Dziadek (jah-dik)- Grandfather.

Europe (Ur-rope)- continent that is the western part of Eurasia.

Ewa (Eev-a)- a popular girl's name in Poland.

Filip (Feel-ip)- a popular boy's name in Poland.

Fryderyk Chopins (Fred-drik Jou-paen)- famous Polish composer who lived in the 1800s.

gnome (nom)- tiny mythical creature that lives underground and creates havoc for humans.

golabki (go-um-kee)- stuffed cabbage, filled with ground meat.

grzybki (gribp-kee)- mushrooms.

Jakub (Ya-coob)- a popular boy's name in Poland.

Karolina (Kar-o-leen-a)- a popular girl's name in Poland.

kotkeczo (ko-tek)- kittycat.

Krakow (Krac-kof)- second largest and old city in Poland.

lalka (lal-ka)- doll.

makaron (mac-kar-on)- noodles.

Mama (Ma-ma)- Mommy.

Marek (Mar-ek)- a popular boy's name in Poland.

marinate (mar-in-ate)- soaking meat, vegetables, or fish in pickling liquid.

mleko (mle-ko)- milk.

migratory (my-gra-tor-ee)- regular movement of birds, usually north to south to nesting places.

misiek (meesh-ek)- a little bear or bear cub.

mythical (myth-i-cal)- a story that comes from a legend.

Nicolaus Copernicus (Nik-co-lai Cop-per-nik)- famous 16th century astronomer who discovered that the sun is the center of our solar system.

parliament (par-lee-ment) - where laws are made for the government.

pierogi (peer-rog-gee)- potato dumplings that are served either boiled or fried.

pilka nozna (pu-ka noz-nah)- football or soccer.

Pokska (Pol-ska)- Poland.

Polanie (Po-la-kee)- what the people who live in Poland are called. Means people who live in an open field.

Republic of Poland (Pol-land)- country in central Europe.

rosol (ro-sool)- chicken soup.

Sawa (Sa-va)- name of the mythical mermaid who married the founder of Warsaw, who created its name.

ser (ser)- cheese.

sklep (skl-ep)- store.

sejm (se-jem)- Parliament.

szkola (sko-wa)- school.

szynca (shin-ka)- ham.

sledz (sle-je)- pickled fish called herring, served with onions and sour cream.

Tata (Ta-ta)- Daddy.

Vistula (Vis-jula)- largest and longest river in Poland.

Wars (Wars)- name of the fisherman who founded the city Warsaw.

Warsaw (Var-shav-a)- capital of Poland.

Wawell (Vav-vel)- legend of a dragon that terrorized the city of Krakow.

Weronika (Ver-on-ee-ka)- a popular girl's name in Poland.

Wielicza (Via-lech-ka) Salt Mine- ancient salt mine that produced table salt up until 2007. It has detailed sculptures and is a great tourist attraction.

Wroclaw (Vro-swaf)- largest city in Western Poland.

zloty (zwa-te)- money.

CPSIA information can be obtained
at www.ICGtesting.com
Printed in the USA
LVHW070000011218
598753LV00007B/28/P

* 9 7 8 1 9 4 7 1 1 8 8 0 5 *